The Book of

The Book of

*Names You Just
Won't Find in
the Other Books!*

DANIEL DAVID

CREATIVE ARTS BOOK COMPANY
Berkeley, California • 1998

The Book of Names
is published by Donald S. Ellis
and distributed by
Creative Arts Book Company.

For information contact:
Creative Arts Book Company
833 Bancroft Way
Berkeley, CA 94710

ISBN 0-88739-173-7
Library of Congress Catalog Number 97-69592

Printed in the United States of America

Dedicated to
My Parents
Venetka & Narsai David

A few notes from the author

- The names are not divided by gender; many of the names can be used for either sex.

- Preferred pronunciation is shown in parenthesis.

- Each first name is shown with a middle and/or last name to emphasize the importance of the marriage between all of the names.

INTRODUCTION

You hold in your hands a book bursting with unique and exciting names. The author has compiled a list of names that you won't find in any other books on the baby name shelf. Some roll off your tongue, some bounce, and some even tap dance. Most, such as **Visolo** and **Koria**, you've never heard before. Others — **Achilles**, **Pierot** — are names that rarely get used today. And still others, such as **Blue** and **Sash**, are words that you've heard in another context, but never would have considered naming your child. **Try thinking of names in a new way.** Don't worry about out-of-date definitions. Try thinking of a name as a dash of color you give to the world; a way to leave your mark, like an elaborate scarf wound through auburn hair, or a periwinkle, paisley tie that everyone admires. You might even find yourself inspired to take one of these names for yourself, not just for your baby!

When you go through this book to find the unique name that's right for your needs, you'll notice that there are no definitions. Why limit yourself by antiquated, arbitrary definitions which in the end, have nothing to do with the child who bears the name? How important is it that Gertrude means "warrior woman" and Michael means "godlike"? Not very. Often a name can mean two different things, maybe "leader" in one language, and "prickly cactus" in another. If you knew that Marion meant "bitter", would you refrain from using it even if it were your favorite name in the world? Of course the meaning wouldn't matter if your heart was set on it. That's why you'll find names on this list which either have no meaning at all or have meaning in another context. It's not important that **Guage** can't be translated. It's not important that **Ajax** can be used in the kitchen and **Minnow** is a fish. **What matters is that you like the name.** Consider going by instinct and choosing names simply because you like the sound! It's okay to trust yourself. You have a creative impulse inside that can guide you to the right name.

Every name we use today has a source. Someone somewhere created each one, and in so doing, added their legacy to our language. At the root of every name lies a spark of inspiration. Now it's your turn to be the author of a name. As parents, who you are as creative individuals will live on in your child. Your personality will be reflected in their name. Giving your children a name from this book will set them apart from all those Elizabeths and Johns. Their name will illuminate their identity in a special way, granting them uniqueness in an overwhelmingly anonymous world. While all the Michaels huddle in a crowd, **Hockney** will glow; **Isola** will sparkle.

Remember, you can always pick a name from this book only as a middle name. If you simply adore the name **Chimmney** but can't bring yourself to use it as a first name, consider calling your kid Jason Chimmney Parker. When he gets tired of common old Jason, he can ask people to start calling him Chimmney. Or you can call your child an unusual first name, but give them a more standard middle name. How about Pasha Jane Sinclair? If she doesn't like being Pasha, she can always use Jane among her peers. There are so many options in the naming process!

Every person with a weird name can tell funny stories about navigating the world with it. They have to repeat it for strangers; they have to spell it out loud; they get called other names or strange hybrids. Kids might snicker or make up nicknames for them. But they can also recount the rewarding experiences that their inventive name has brought them. Every time they have to spell or repeat their name to a stranger, they open the door into a conversation with someone they would not have ordinarily talked to. Every time their name gets mispronounced, they get asked curious questions and are paid extra attention. And, every time someone dubs them a funny nickname, they also receive countless compliments from those conventionally named folks who covet their originality. They might even find that an unusual name benefits them in ways they never could have imagined. Consider what happened to a small girl with a peculiar name on the first day of school:

Mr. O'Neill swayed slowly from the heels to the balls of his feet; his thick, stubby fingers grasping firmly to either side of the faux-wood podium. With jowls and a mouth set like a bulldog, he fixed his hard eyes of the seventh grade class and called the roll on this first day of school. One little girl sat tensely, waiting for her strange name to come booming across the classroom. Mr.

O'Neill was already at the M's.

"Jennifer Morris!" he bellowed.

A hand crept slowly up. "Here", peeped a girl a few chairs ahead.

"Adam O'Connor."

A tough guy slouching in his seat muttered, "Yeh, here..."

"Sit up straight!" ordered Mr. O'Neill. The boy snapped to attention.

"Laura Parks."

"Present," whispered someone in the back row.

"Speak up! barked the teacher.

"Pre...present," spoke the voice, a tad bit louder.

Suddenly, Mr. O'Neill fell silent. He was staring intently at his roll call sheet, so intently that the whole class could see the top of his head and the circle near the back where his military regime haircut grew sparse. He kept staring down at the page. Tiny beads of sweat gathered at his temples. His fingers drummed nervously on the podium. With his right hand, he yanked at his brown, polyester pants. His nose twitched. A minute passed. The class began to stir. What could be the matter?

The little girl knew she was the only one who could help him.

"Um, I think the next one, it might be me," she stammered.

Mr. O'Neill glanced up and looked straight at her.

She spoke: "Lilan... You say Leelawn Pahtree." She looked quickly down at here desk.

Mr. O'Neill paused. And then, for the first time that morning there was a softness in his voice. "Thanks," he muttered humbly. "Lilan." His stern gaze melted. He smiled at her.

She smiled back.

"Kenneth Rogers!" he yelled.

The little girl was me twelve years ago. It wasn't always easy to have this name. But on that day in Mr. O'Neill's class I learned that "Lilan" had a certain power not shared by the Kenneths, Lauras, Adams and Jennifers of the world. To think a name could be funky and ingenious enough to sweeten up even a drill sergeant of a teacher! This book is full of names just like that. Don't confine your offspring to the dull majority. Let **Heron** and **Paradiso** work their magic!

Take a good look at these names. Some you'll laugh at. Some you'll think silly or bizarre. But you may come across a name — either as rare as **Rhone** or as unconventional as **Bilt** — and pause for a second to say, "Hey, I like the sound of that, how cool!" And you may just like it enough to daringly rename yourself or offer your child the gift of an extraordinary name.

Good luck on a lively journey into the fertile world of NAMES, where, from the words and sounds of our surroundings, these names were harvested from the richest of crops. Pleasant pickings!

Lilan Patri

NAMES

A.C.
> Ex: *A.C. Carey Reynolds*

Aalten
> (ALL-TIN)
> Ex: *Aalten Perrin Smith*

Azzarei
> (AS-ARE-AY)
> Ex: *Azzarei Roland Bechtel*

Abacus
> Ex: *Abacus Wen Stevens*

Abile
> (A-BILL)
> Ex: *Abile Maddie Ryanson*

Absinthe
> Ex: *Absinthe Chester Malone*

Acacia
> Ex: *Acacia Rose Sullivan*

Acadia
> Ex: *Acadia Cole Baxter*

Acara
> (AH-CAR-AH)
> Ex: *Acara Nellie Smith*

Acari
> (AH-CAR-IE)
> Ex: *Acari Crosby Stills*

Acaru
> (A-CAR-OO)
> Ex: *Acaru Wills Jameson*

Achilles
> Ex: *Achilles Sample Hellerson*

Achim
> (AH-KEEM)
> Ex: *Achim Allen Lewis*

Acton
> Ex: *Acton Roland Stilles*

Adaline
> Ex: *Adaline Lewis Stevenson*

Adella
> Ex: *Adella Marie Martinez*

Adina
> (AH-DEE-NA)
> Ex: *Adina Rosa Alvarez*

Adlar
> Ex: *Adlar Allen Jones*

Aeolus
> (AY-O-LUS)
> Ex: *Aeolus Whalen Pitman*

Aero
> Ex: *Aero Jacob Starr*

Aeron
> (AIR-ON)
> Ex: *Aeron Nicholas Bailer*

Agius
> (AY-JUSS)
> Ex: *Agius Matthew Taylor*

Ahramis
> (UH-RAY-MISS)
> Ex: *Ahramis Cole Nexler*

Aileen
> (AY-LEAN)
> Ex: *Aileen Vella Stoker*

Ainsley
> Ex: *Ainsley Paula Matson*

Airel
> Ex: *Airel Daylin Jones*

Aitor
> (AY-TORE)
> Ex: *Aitor Nathan Cain*

Ajax
> Ex: *Ajax Marcus Weston*

Ake
> Ex: *Ake Willis Peterson*

Alabama
> Ex: *Alabama Silvi Dyer*

Aladdin
>Ex: *Aladdin Todd Greene*

Albany
>Ex: *Sue Albany Watson*

Albion
>Ex: *Albion Rice Wexler*

Alcala
>Ex: *Alcala Rivera Beatty*

Alcatraz
>Ex: *Christopher Alcatraz Cobbler*

Aldagrove
>Ex: *Aldagrove Rhen Stevens*

Aldea
>Ex: *Tammy Aldea Farnsworth*

Alder
>Ex: *Alder Bixby Matson*

Aldo
>Ex: *Aldo Allen Courtland*

Alejo
>(AL-AY-HO)
>Ex: *Jake Alejo Stevens*

Alesian
>(AL-EE-SHIN)
>Ex: *Alesian Ramon Vexler*

Alger
>(AL-JUR)
>Ex: *Marcus Alger Callahan*

Algier
>(AL-JEER)
>Ex: *Algier Willis Babcock*

Alinda
>Ex: *Sherry Alinda Bryerson*

Alinka
>Ex: *Karen Alinka Porter*

Alloy
>Ex: *Christian Alloy Miller*

Aloe
> Ex: *Aloe Carey Shores*

Alpha
> Ex: *Alpha Radley Mitchell*

Alpine
> Ex: *Carey Alpine Pearly*

Alta
> Ex: *Paula Alta Graff*

Alton
> Ex: *Tony Alton Greer*

Alves
> Ex: *Richards Alves Thorinton*

Alluma
> Ex: *Alluma Rose Sonning*

Amador
> Ex: *Amador Christian Stilles*

Amaryllis
> Ex: *Amaryllis Christal Sharp*

Amato
> (AH-MA-TOE)
> Ex: *Amato Dale Stevens*

Ambrose
> Ex: *Ambrose Willis Bolton*

Ambrosia
> Ex: *Ambrosia Alysa Waters*

Amerca
> (AH-MARE-KA)
> Ex: *Amerca Jane Sarrison*

America
> Ex: *Samuel America Payton*

Amerigo
> Ex: *Manuel Amerigo Valdez*

Amethyst
> Ex: *Amethyst Raquel Pittford*

Amir
> (AH-MEER)
> Ex: *Jaylin Amir Razzami*

Amos
Ex: *Vincent Amos Allen*
Andros
Ex: *Mark Andros Parker*
Anemone
(AH-NEM-OH-NEE)
Ex: *Susan Anemone Stone*
Angora
Ex: *Angora Roxanne Smith*
Anisetta
Ex: *Roseyln Anisetta Marianos*
Annadale
Ex: *Annadale Elizabeth Radley*
Anniston
Ex: *Rex Anniston Portier*
Anselmo
Ex: *Steven Anselmo Jones*
Antelope
Ex: *Antelope Ramona Ramirez*
Antigo
Ex: *Raull Antigo Santiago*
Antigua
(ANN-TEE-GWA)
Ex: *Antigua Susana Callista*
Aoki
(AY-OH-KEY)
Ex: *Aoki Gin Roberts*
Aptos
Ex: *Todd Aptos Wheeler*
Aqua
Ex: *Aqua Nicole Fisher*
Aquavit
(AH-KWA-VEET)
Ex: *Aquavit Cannon Calder*
Arabian
Ex: *Bailey Arabian Buchannan*

Aragon
>(AIR-AH-GONE)
>Ex: *Aragon Carrey Smith*

Aram
>Ex: *Aram Craig Aiken*

Arca
>Ex: *Arca Suzanne Walton*

Arcy
>Ex: *Alexandria Arcy Courtland*

Arena
>Ex: *Arena Michelle Gainor*

Argent
>Ex: *Samuel Argent Taylor*

Arglyle
>Ex: *Susan Arglye Smith*

Arkansas
>Ex: *Jack Arkansas Swensen*

Arleta
>(AR-LET-TA)
>Ex: *Tania Arleta Weston*

Arley
>Ex: *Arley Cole Thompson*

Armitage
>Ex: *Jane Armitage Sansome*

Artic
>Ex: *Artic Rail Cogsworth*

Artino
>Ex: *Artino Ricardo Sails*

Aruba
>Ex: *Donna Aruba Gates*

Arvada
>(AR-VAY-DA)
>Ex: *Corrina Arvada Ramirez*

Arzat
>Ex: *Arzat Thomas Smith*

Ashby
>Ex: *Ashby Nicole Street*

Asher
Ex: *Johnny Asher Baker*
Ashford
Ex: *Ashford Rex Billings*
Ashlan
Ex: *Rachel Ashlan Tiddings*
Ashur
Ex: *Ashur Graecano*
Ashwood
Ex: *Paul Ashwood Sandler*
Asta
Ex: *Asta Jones*
Aster
Ex: *Aster Pixley Robertson*
Astin
Ex: *Vespa Astin Pelligrini*
Astor
Ex: *Kim Astor Rogers*
Astron
Ex: *Rex Astron Evanston*
Athens
Ex: *Tamara Athens Rosenthal*
Atkin
Ex: *Atkin Torrence Jackson*
Atlanta
Ex: *Atlanta Lynn Stevenson*
Atlantic
Ex: *Robert Atlantic Cain*
Atlin
Ex: *Toby Atlin James*
Atmos
Ex: *Atmos Ryan Mattson*
Attalla
Ex: *Erica Attalla Ryerson*
Aubin
(OH-BIN)
Ex: *Aubin Jones*

Auborn

   Ex: *Jane Auborn Sinclair*

Aurora

   Ex: *Nina Aurora Stevenson*

Ava

   (AY-VA)

   Ex: *Ava Pearl*

Avalon

   Ex: *Rick Avalon Sampson*

Avant

   (AH-VAHNT)

   Ex: *Avant Marina Jacard*

Avedon

   (AH-VEH-DAWN)

   Ex: *Zane Avedon Spear*

Avenida

   Ex: *Avenida Laura Smith*

Avian

   Ex: *Alexis Avian Kimball*

Avianca

   (AH-VI-ON-KA)

   Ex: *Avianca Ambrose Sanchez*

Avila

   (AH-VEE-LA)

   Ex: *Lexi Avila McKinney*

Avin

   Ex: *Avin Gerrund Jones*

Avion

   Ex: *Alexander Avion Ail*

Avirita

   Ex: *Avirita Rose*

Avondale

   Ex: *Zachery Avondale Spencer*

Avril

   Ex: *Avril Peters*

Axel

   Ex: *Axel Sin Joiner*

Axis
>Ex: *Axis Mary Marino*

Ay
>Ex: *Ay Perry Rizen*

Ayala
>(I-ALL-A)
>Ex: *Ayala Donna Moore*

Ayenee
>Ex: *Ayenee Sara McNair*

Ayler
>Ex: *Ayler Ryland Sloan*

Aylor
>Ex: *Rick Aylor Bekins*

Aymax
>Ex: *Roufus Aymax Bixler*

Ayr
>Ex: *Tom Ayr Wexler*

Azalia
>Ex: *Azalia Ann Burlin*

Azevedo
>(AS-EH-VAY-DOE)
>Ex: *Bobby Azevedo Anders*

Azores
>Ex: *Azores Evan Cole*

B

Ex: *B Waitlin Mines*

Baba

Ex: *Baba Haddad*

Bacall

Ex: *Bacall Betsy Peterson*

Bacardi

Ex: *Barcardi Willis Jenkins*

Baffin

Ex: *Sam Baffin Wilson*

Bahama

Ex: *Andreas Bahama Cooper*

Bailen

Ex: *Bailen Moore Ryerson*

Baja

Ex: *Jack Baja Dune*

Balboa

Ex: *Lisa Balboa Walton*

Balen

(BAA-LEN)

Ex: *Balen Michael Gore*

Balentine

Ex: *Stephanie Balentine Diamond*

Ballon

Ex: *Panther Ballon Phillips*

Baltic

Ex: *Baltic Jones*

Bamboo

Ex: *Bamboo Soren Sinclair*

Banbury

Ex: *Sarah Banbury Wills*

Bancroft

Ex: *Bancroft Jerrund Beales*

Bandelaire

Ex: *Ricky Bandelaire Borrinson*

Banguard

Ex: *Morris Banguard Walker*

Banks
> Ex: *Banks Cohen Fisher*

Baptiste
> Ex: *Jean Baptiste Mission*

Barbados
> Ex: *Malcolm Barbados Michner*

Barbano
> (BAR-BAH-NO)
> Ex: *Vince Barbano Bail*

Barbee
> Ex: *Barbee Bell*

Barbera
> Ex: *Jules Barbera Cox*

Barbuda
> Ex: *Barbuda Bronks*

Barn
> Ex: *Barn Barron Gainor*

Barnum
> Ex: *Bill Barnum Staples*

Bartel
> Ex: *Marcus Bartel DelSanto*

Bartlett
> Ex: *Sarah Bartlett Pearson*

Barton
> Ex: *Christopher Barton Steele*

Baru
> Ex: *Spaniel Baru Jones*

Basco
> Ex: *Dwayne Basco Price*

Bassett
> Ex: *Silvia Bassett Akeman*

Bassie
> Ex: *Bassie Monroe*

Batelin
> Ex: *Lisa Batelin Robins*

Bates
> Ex: *Aurthur Bates Topella*

Batori

Ex: *Batori Norland*

Bautista

Ex: *Bautista Parker Burns*

Bax

Ex: *Bax Taylin*

Bayaka

Ex: *Cindy Bayaka Sanderson*

Baye

Ex: *Baye Seton Wallace*

Bayes

Ex: *Bayes d'Or Railand*

Baylor

Ex: *Baylor Lane Bexler*

Beacon

Ex: *Beacon Todd Silver*

Beale

Ex: *Beale Sarrington Moore*

Bechor

(BECK-OR)

Ex: *Bechor John*

Bechtel

Ex: *Phoebe Bechtel Sails*

Becker

Ex: *Shelby Becker Willits*

Beech

Ex: *Brandon Beech Tillman*

Beeini

(BEE-EN-EE)

Ex: *Beeini Sales Cartwright*

Beem

Ex: *Nicholas Beem Price*

Beienel

(BEE-EN-ELLE)

Ex: *Beienel Stevens*

Beijing

Ex: *Beijing Li Thompson*

Belaire

Ex: *Spencer Belaire Robbins*

Beldin

Ex: *Robert Beldin Stark*

Beldon

Ex: *Macy Beldon Clark*

Belize

Ex: *Elizabeth Belize Brighton*

Belmont

Ex: *Belmont Sheraton*

Beltine

Ex: *Jason Beltine Walker*

Belvedere

Ex: *Belvedere Marie Presley*

Benbow

Ex: *Rodney Benbow Rodriguiz*

Bendel

Ex: *Bendel Wyman Wilks*

Bendix

Ex: *Bendix Ruben Parker*

Bennet

Ex: *Jessica Bennet Fox*

Bengal

Ex: *Bengal Lloyd Webster*

Bento

Ex: *John Bento Price*

Benton

Ex: *Benton Wayne Wilson*

Beo

Ex: *Beo Connor Millens*

Beowolf

Ex: *Charles Beowolf Excaliber*

Berent

Ex: *William Berent Brice*

Bergen
Ex: *Bergen Tye Sallinger*
Bering
Ex: *Bering Nealand Solari*
Beringer
Ex: *Thomas Beringer Appleby*
Berman
Ex: *Victor Berman Johnson*
Beston
Ex: *Chet Beston Bearman*
Beta
Ex: *Randolf Beta Chartes*
Bexley
Ex: *Bexley Avin Moore*
Bicksley
Ex: *Bicksley Trevor Holmes*
Billings
Ex: *Darrin Billings Connors*
Bilt
Ex: *Bilt Steven Ryerson*
Biltmore
Ex: *Biltmore Jackson Bird*
Bioletti
Ex: *Jacqueline Bioletti Smith*
Bionda
Ex: *Bionda Paisley Grey*
Birley
Ex: *Birley Blithe Halloway*
Birmingham
Ex: *Carla Birmingham Barthe*
Bisbee
Ex: *Ona Bisbee Dale*
Bisco
Ex: *Bisco May Peerman*
Bisquo
Ex: *Jay Bisquo Pierce*

Bizou
Ex: *Lola Bizou Branca*
Bjork
Ex: *Bjork Conrad Skores*
Bobo
Ex: *Bobo Jack Rillin*
Bogard
Ex: *Gallen Bogard Giles*
Bogie
Ex: *Bogie Anders Cole*
Bolero
Ex: *Sam Bolero Bryerson*
Bolinger
Ex: *Chloe Bolinger Bricks*
Bolt
Ex: *Bolt Sheldon*
Bolton
Ex: *Wilks Bolton Kellen*
Bombay
Ex: *Salina Bombay Junips*
Bond
Ex: *Bond Era Ricks*
Bonsai
Ex: *Jerret Bonsai Kale*
Bonta
Ex: *Shirley Bonta Kaye*
Booth
Ex: *Booth Ales Wilt*
Bora
Ex: *Bora Bora Bronks*
Bordean
Ex: *Bordean Rice Becker*
Bosch
Ex: *Bosch Hollis*
Bose
(BOZE)
Ex: *Bose Allison Rand*

Boston
>Ex: *Leo Boston Varella*

Bourne
>Ex: *Leonard Bourne Balice*

Bova
>Ex: *Bova Reeves*

Bovo
>Ex: *Bovo Richards Gellin*

Boxer
>Ex: *Boxer Cravates*

Bracano
>Ex: *Julio Bracano Broussard*

Braemar
>Ex: *Braemar Lindo Fierendino*

Brahm
>Ex: *Brahm Riley Santos*

Brando
>Ex: *Tare Brando Shields*

Branwyn
>Ex: *Jill Branwyn Pinkerton*

Brazen
>Ex: *Brazen Rich Evans*

Bree
>Ex: *Carla Bree Seens*

Brekken
>Ex: *Brekken Stiles Tate*

Bremen
>Ex: *Vic Bremen Goldman*

Bremmen
>Ex: *Youri Bremmen Volcari*

Breton
>Ex: *Breton Morecroft*

Brewster
>Ex: *Milvin Brewster Phillips*

Briar
>Ex: *Leena Briar Sorrinson*

Briarcliff
> Ex: *Eric Briarcliff Staten*

Brice
> Ex: *Brice Marina Hane*

Brick
> Ex: *Brick Conrad Fishell*

Bricka
> Ex: *Bricka Lesley Thomas*

Bridges
> Ex: *Madison Bridges Wright*

Brighton
> Ex: *Brighton Tenor Phillips*

Brinell
> Ex: *Brinell Esther Wilson*

Brinks
> Ex: *Torina Brinks Fierce*

Briones
> (BREE-O-NEEZE)
> Ex: *Felicia Briones Brown*

Brisbane
> Ex: *Xavier Brisbane Cordovino*

Brisdale
> Ex: *Sarah Brisdale Phoenix*

Bristol
> Ex: *Carrie Bristol Wallace*

Briston
> Ex: *Sylvia Briston Sanders*

Brive
> Ex: *Randall Brive Welks*

Brix
> Ex: *Brix Brody*

Brockton
> Ex: *Raquel Brockton Stone*

Brooklyn
> Ex: *Cedric Brooklyn Isles*

Brubeck
> Ex: *Jorin Brubeck Giles*

Bryce
Ex: *Leon Bryce Saber*
Buckeye
Ex: *Buckeye Kirtland*
Buick
Ex: *Roland Buick VanBuhler*
Bulgaria
Ex: *Valin Bulgaria Rix*
Buren
(BJURE-IN)
Ex: *Sibbel Buren Cains*
Burlin
Ex: *Burlin Colton Vandenbosch*
Buzby
Ex: *Buzby Vierra*
Buzz
Ex: *Buzz Sales*
Byer
Ex: *Noland Byer Wright*
Byrd
(BIRD)
Ex: *Byrd Sellice Stare*
Byxbee
Ex: *Byxbee Steeles*

C
> Ex: *C Trenor Cohen*

Caan
> Ex: *Caan Clorox Coleman*

Cabri
> Ex: *Cabri Tiles Walker*

Cache
> Ex: *Cache Steven Walton*

Cactus
> Ex: *Cactus Karen Teales*

Cade
> Ex: *Cade Willis Toland*

Cadell
> Ex: *Cadell Milt Tyland*

Cadet
> Ex: *Cadet Walker Thomas*

Caetano
> (KAY-TA-NO)
> Ex: *Caetano Michelle Torinelli*

Cahlia
> (KA-LEE-A)
> Ex: *Cahlia Nelly Marcello*

Caige
> Ex: *Caige Julan Dorlanski*

Caine
> Ex: *Caine Wexler Krinski*

Cairns
> Ex: *Cairns Mae Kotovsky*

Cairo
> Ex: *Cairo Sin Rallencourt*

Calan
> Ex: *Calan Marcus Christoff*

Calico
> Ex: *Calico Torrie Lowery*

California
> Ex: *California Stevens*

Calin
> Ex: *Calin Serin Thomas*

Calista
> Ex: *Calista Marie Genetti*

Calistoga
> Ex: *Calistoga Henni Stiles*

Calix
> Ex: *Calix Jay Imura*

Callia
> Ex: *Callia Wexford Ikes*

Calloway
> Ex: *Calloway Berin Tales*

Calypso
> Ex: *Jorin Calypso Ikeda*

Calyptus
> Ex: *Calyptus Connie Hale*

Calyx
> Ex: *Calyx Lauren Moreida*

Camden
> Ex: *Camden Milen Jones*

Campari
> Ex: *Campari Emin Vallenstone*

Canada
> Ex: *Canada Lane Montgomery*

Cannon
> Ex: *John Cannon Jeffries*

Cano
> (KAY-NO)
> Ex: *Cano Oscar Morano*

Canoe
> Ex: *Canoe Francisco Siquedis*

Canon
> Ex: *Canon Lising Gainor*

Cantor
> Ex: *Cantor Ibarra Huntington*

Canyon
> Ex: *Canyon Sara Harrington*

Caples
> Ex: *Sylvia Caples Price*

Caranda
> Ex: *Caranda Marie Hiranza*

Caravel
> Ex: *Caravel Stevens*

Carib
> Ex: *Carib Bailen Harcourt*

Carline
> Ex: *Carline Carolyn Dvorsky*

Carma
> Ex: *Carma Lynn Dorrentile*

Carmine
> Ex: *Carmine Pritchard*

Carnet
> Ex: *Carnet Rose Osoria*

Carrington
> Ex: *Carrington Steiner Sills*

Carrisa
> Ex: *Carrisa Soreen Duval*

Cartouce
> Ex: *Cartouce Avila Sassano*

Casco
> Ex: *Casco Marin Winfield*

Caselli
> Ex: *Caselli Jane Torrence*

Cashmere
> Ex: *Cashmere Rolls*

Casino
> Ex: *Casino T Wexford*

Cassel
> Ex: *Cassel Leah Ferrington*

Cassia
> Ex: *Cassia Jillan Kales*

Catala
> Ex: *Catala Line Azevedo*

Catalia
> Ex: *Catalia Loren Illando*

Cavel
> Ex: *Cavel Whitmore Thomas*

Caven
> Ex: *Caven Dallen Tares*

Cavon
> Ex: *Cavon Smiley Spears*

Cayes
> Ex: *Cayes Smith*

Cayman
> Ex: *Valerie Cayman Baboolovitch*

Cayne
> Ex: *Cayne Aylin Seales*

Cea
> (SAY-UH)
> Ex: *Cea Miles Chang*

Cedar
> Ex: *Cedar Ray Chetkovich*

Celadon
> Ex: *Robert Celandon Eschellman*

Cerro
> Ex: *Cerro Ethridge Wales*

Cerulean
> Ex: *Cerulean Palm*

Ceryle
> (SARE-ULL)
> Ex: *Ceryle Jane Wexford*

Cessna
> Ex: *Cessna C Lee*

Ceylon
> Ex: *Ceylon Iwataki*

Cezanne
> Ex: Cezanne Cantacello Chagall
> Ex: *Delano Chagall Writman*

Chaise
> Ex: *Chaise Alice Dain*

Chanterelle
Ex: *Chanterelle Marilyn Leonetta*
Chantrey
Ex: *Chantrey Anne Durantine*
Chartreuse
Ex: *Chartreuse Giovella*
Chase
Ex: *Chase Perrin Thompson*
Chavall
Ex: *Lauren Chavall Pritton*
Cheetah
Ex: *Cheetah Montgomery*
Chelo
Ex: *Chelo Perrin Payne*
Cheney
Ex: *Cheney Riles Jorgenson*
Chettah
Ex: *Chettah Jack*
Chevron
Ex: *Chevron Jordan Collins*
Cheyenne
Ex: *Samantha Cheyenne Colanson*
Chianti
Ex: *Chianti Belle Marlena*
Chiarello
Ex: *Chiarello Roland Marlentono*
Chime
Ex: *Chime Susan Paddington*
Chimmney
Ex: *Chimmney Toland Rhomberg*
Chinex
Ex: *Chinex T Richardson*
Chiron
Ex: *Chiron Page Williford*
Chisel
Ex: *Chisel Stallworth*

Chisholm
> Ex: *Rex Chisholm Weldencour*

Chivallo
> Ex: *Chivallo C Errinson*

Choco
> Ex: *Choco Rodriguez*

Christele
> Ex: *Christele Marie Korvinovitch*

Chrome
> Ex: *Chrome Baker*

Chrysler
> Ex: *Chrysler T Bookland*

Ciente
> (CEE-EN-TEE)
> Ex: *Ciente Railin Sorentis*

Cinder
> Ex: *Cinder Coland Sandelco*

Cisco
> Ex: *Cisco Bryer Robertson*

Citrus
> Ex: *Citrus Norland Brightenson*

Civa
> Ex: *Civa Paulna Lerrinfjord*

Claesz
> (CLAYS)
> Ex: *Claesz Roland Sankovich*

Claremont
> Ex: *Julie Claremont Reid*

Claret
> Ex: *Claret Virin Colbrin*

Clarinda
> Ex: *Clarinda Vellis Satomi*

Clem
> Ex: *Clem T Marcovich*

Clemence
> Ex: *Clemence Aaron Vallentole*

Cleto
(CLAY-TOE)
Ex: *Cleto Peters Stevens*

Clifton
Ex: *Clifton Jalice Pallerton*

Cline
Ex: *Cline Waler Hunterton*

Clone
Ex: *Clone C Pixford*

Clove
Ex: *Clove Eastons Phillips*

Clydesdale
Ex: *Julie Clydesdale Walker*

Coad
Ex: *Coad Maxton Zillman*

Coast
Ex: *Coast Emily Syers*

Cobalt
Ex: *Bexler Cobalt Black*

Cochran
Ex: *Jaron Cochran Sails*

Coda
Ex: *Coda Stiles*

Codex
Ex: *Codex Martinoff*

Cohiba
Ex: *Cohiba Anne Lexington*

Colan
Ex: *Colan Robert Goldstone*

Colby
Ex: *Colby Cherin Villentoy*

Cole
Ex: *Cole Jackson*

Colston
Ex: *Colston Wexford Appleby*

Colton
Ex: *Colton Sorenti Carontonella*

Coltrane
> Ex: *Jack Coltrane Sacks*

Colusa
> Ex: *Colusa Rebecca Johnston*

Coney
> Ex: *Coney Marta Gulbrandsen*

Confetti
> Ex: *Confetti Anna Tanson*

Congo
> Ex: *Congo Ryanson*

Conifer
> Ex: *Roland Conifer Walker*

Connecticut
> Ex: *Connecticut Jones*

Connel
> Ex: *Samuel Connel Hatson*

Connolly
> Ex: *Jill Connolly Max*

Conroe
> Ex: *Conroe Marton Smith*

Consuelo
> Ex: *Consuelo Maria Corinna*

Copine
> Ex: *Copine Andrew Bondes*

Coppola
> Ex: *Darwin Coppola Dales*

Coral
> Ex: *Coral Franchesca Mareno*

Corbett
> Ex: *Corbett Baxter Bails*

Cordele
> Ex: *Cordele Rainy Nexford*

Corinthe
> Ex: *Corinthe Anne Phillips*

Corion
> Ex: *Corion Bix Styford*

Corlee
>   Ex: *Corlee Laura Lee*

Corlita
>   Ex: *Corlita Maria Vinticella*

Corlon
>   Ex: *Derrin Colon Giles*

Cornet
>   Ex: *Cornet Stevens*

Corniche
>   Ex: *Corniche Madella Sarrento*

Corolla
>   Ex: *Corolla Seico*

Corona
>   Ex: *Stella Corona Stoleno*

Corsair
>   Ex: *Corsair Day Ennington*

Corsica
>   Ex: *Corsica Jane Sovento*

Corsican
>   Ex: *Rex Corsican Sane*

Cortex
>   Ex: *Joran Cortex Lexton*

Cortola
>   Ex: *Cortola Mae DiCenza*

Cosby
>   Ex: *Cosby Daylin Ford*

Cosmo
>   Ex: *Cosmo T Worrenton*

Costello
>   Ex: *Costello Salino Rivera*

Cove
>   Ex: *Cove Waldon*

Covey
>   Ex: *Covey C Rains*

Covin
>   Ex: *Covin Walker Tapes*

Coy
>Ex: *Coy Day Osborne*

Coyle
>Ex: *Coyle T Wexler*

Coyote
>Ex: *Coyote Phillips*

Crane
>Ex: *Jacqueline Crane Sarringston*

Creole
>Ex: *Creole Batchelor Scott*

Crimson
>Ex: *Crimson Berrin Sills*

Curry
>Ex: *Curry Amy Millen*

Cristalle
>Ex: *Cristalle Rose Hyzer*

Crivello
>Ex: *Crivello Black Domingo*

Crosby
>Ex: *Crosby Ashford Jakes*

Curran
>Ex: *Curran Rose Isquierda*

Cutter
>Ex: *Cutter Thompson Tyes*

Cyan
>(SIGH-ANN)
>Ex: *Cyan Jack Jones*

Cyber
>Ex: *Cyber J Cain*

Cyrano
>Ex: *Cyrano T Wintercole*

Cyrene
>Ex: *Cyrene Tara Smith*

Cysco
>Ex: *Cysco Vallens Enjala*

D
> Ex: *D Terrin Silton*

D.C.
> Ex: *D.C. Lou Tarton*

Dagger
> Ex: *Dagger Q Maxton*

Dagget
> Ex: *Dagget Steener Thomas*

Dailin
> Ex: *Dailin Extin Roebin*

Dako
> Ex: *Dako Bitto Tykes*

Dakota
> Ex: *Dakota Tonin Riter*

Dalea
> (DAY-LEE-UH)
> Ex: *Daylea Raykin Santos*

Dali
> (DOLLY)
> Ex: *Dali Catalin Pellor*

Dane
> Ex: *Dane Wilton Pile*

Danko
> Ex: *Danko Cains*

Danridge
> Ex: *Danridge Wilson Merikan*

Dash
> Ex: *Dash Errand*

Dashwood
> Ex: *Dashwood Willis Tones*

Davia
> Ex: *Davia Bassil Fillant*

Davos
> (DAYVOS or DAH-VOS)
> Ex: *Jallin Davos Smith*

Dayouai
> (DAY-OO-I)
> Ex: *Dayouai Jane Corstan*

Dax
> Ex: *Dax Cherrin Walker*

Dayao
> (DAY-O)
> Ex: *Dayao Salin More*

Daytona
> Ex: *Daytona Jail Corsithe*

Deakin
> Ex: *Deakin Jones*

Decca
> Ex: *Decca Sarah Smokes*

Decco
> Ex: *Decco Day Blige*

December
> Ex: *December Staples*

Deiniol
> (DAY-IN-EE-OL)
> Ex: *Deiniol Cartoon Songsworth*

Deisel
> Ex: *Deisel Cross*

Dela
> (DAY-LA)
> Ex: *Sophia Dela Costa*

Delaine
> Ex: *Delaine Silton Miles*

Delana
> (DA-LAY-NA)
> Ex: *Delana Rae Cartwright*

Delaney
> Ex: *Delaney Sints Topelin*

Delano
> Ex: *Delano Corrin Stevens*

Delft
> Ex: *Delft Roybin Fents*

Delia
>   Ex: *Delia Sarts Ritz*

Delmar
>   Ex: *Delmar Berrin Tye*

Delox
>   Ex: *Delox Boxer Boyle*

Delphine
>   Ex: *Vena Delphine Aints*

Delphinium
>   Ex: *Suzanne Delphinium Wirn*

Delray
>   Ex: *Delray Walker*

Delta
>   Ex: *Delta Sebrin Fikes*

Deluna
>   Ex: *Juliana Deluna Korinski*

Delwood
>   Ex: *Max Delwood Beens*

Denio
>   Ex: *Denio Bye Cortes*

Dennett
>   Ex: *Dennett Bilston Blike*

Denslowe
>   Ex: *Stuart Denslowe Giles*

Denver
>   Ex: *Denver Jana Jefferson*

Derby
>   Ex: *Porche Derby Emerson*

Dermit
>   Ex: *Dermit Townsend*

Dero
>   Ex: *Zachery Dero Sorringson*

Derringer
>   Ex: *Zoe Derringer Whites*

Desert
>   Ex: *Susie Desert Rain*

D

Desoto
>Ex: *Desoto Baxter Nells*

Detoro
>Ex: *Detoro Bolts Black*

Detroit
>Ex: *Detroit Stevens*

Deuce
>Ex: *Deuce Kix*

Devons
>Ex: *Devons Chester Malone*

Dice
>Ex: *Dice Bricks*

Dideon
>Ex: *Dideon Jacobs*

Diehl
>(DEAL)
>Ex: *Diehl Dalila Doll*

Diem
>Ex: *Diem Gordon Charts*

Dieval
>(DEE-VULL)
>Ex: *Rochele Dieval Morgan*

Digit
>Ex: *Digit Cato Richmond*

Dine
>Ex: *Dine Erriks Dates*

Dingo
>Ex: *Dingo Datsun*

Dino
>Ex: *Dino Fornelli Salerno*

Dira
>Ex: *Dira Siya Sanes*

Discin
>Ex: *Discin Satcliff*

Disco
>Ex: *Disco Bixler Wayne*

Disney
  Ex: *Disney Jane Carrington*
Dita
  Ex: *Dita Rose*
Ditto
  Ex: *Ditto Ray Johnson*
Divine
  Ex: *Jill Divine Black*
Dizzy
  Ex: *Dizzy Wexler Phillips*
Djourne
  Ex: *Djourne Sintro Sails*
Docena
  Ex: *Docena Marie Corlando*
Dohn
  (DOAN)
  Dohn Jakes
Doll
  Ex: *Doll Gypsie Wakes*
Dolland
  Ex: *Dolland Basco Wrights*
Dominica
  Ex: *Dominica Rae Costillo*
Domino
  Ex: *Domino Factor Price*
Donegan
  Ex: *Donegan Bailey McKinnon*
Donner
  Ex: *Sylvia Donner Rhodes*
Dorado
  Ex: *Dorado Rachel Alexis*
Doric
  Ex: *Doric Rick Ales*
Dory
  Ex: *Dory Chitin Sales*
Dox
  Ex: *Dox Walker*

Doyle
Ex: *Doyle Jenner Tomms*
Drago
Ex: *Drago Cranston Sikes*
Dresden
Ex: *Dresden Saron Timton*
Drexel
Ex: *Drexel Lurey Finns*
Driscoll
Ex: *Driscoll Stevens*
Dryden
Ex: *Dryden Dailin Bronks*
Dubbs
Ex: *Ryan Dubbs Dyne*
Dumosa
Ex: *Dumosa Tina Kintall*
Dundes
Ex: *Dundes John Stone*
Dune
Ex: *Dune Rakin Cranes*
Dupont
Ex: *Dupont Brighton Price*
Durango
Ex: *Durango Langston Plains*
Durham
Ex: *Durham Berrin Black*
Duvall
Ex: *Joseph Duvall Modello*
Duveen
Ex: *Duveen Jensen*

E
>Ex: *E Landor Erill*

Eames
>Ex: *Eames Peerson*

Early
>Ex: *Early Cheeks*

Easson
>(EE-SON)
>Ex: *Easson Tiner Take*

East
>Ex: *East Base Texlyn*

Easton
>Ex: *Easton Wakes*

Eaton
>Ex: *Eaton John Wallace*

Eves
>*Eves Bain Casssil*

Ebbet
>Ex: *Ebbet Brubeck Caid*

Echto
>Ex: *Echto Zydo Core*

Edenton
>Ex: *Edenton Whisko Fent*

Edsel
>Ex: *Edsel Bryerson Akhotani*

Egypt
>Ex: *Lauren Egypt Paikes*

Eich
>Ex: *Eich Rin Weyton*

Eiffel
>(EYE-FILL)
>Ex: *Sara Eiffel Davis*

Elecka
>Ex: *Elecka Raine*

Electra
>Ex: *Electra Bates*

Eleno
> (EL-AY-NO)
> Ex: *Eleno Cortex*

Elgin
> Ex: *Lorissa Elgin Cycourt*

Elk
> Ex: *Elk Dindo Brooks*

Elkus
> Ex: *Elkus Finns*

Elle
> Ex: *Elle Sarta*

Ellington
> Ex: *Jake Ellington Paston*

Elmont
> Ex: *Elmont Kingston*

Elmwood
> Ex: *Elmwood Riles*

Ember
> Ex: *Susan Ember Brakeston*

Emileen
> Ex: *Emileen Sue Pritchford*

Emmet
> Ex: *Emmet Phillip Lynch*

Encino
> Ex: *Encino Straws*

Enez
> (EE-NEZ)
> Ex: *Enez Pixton Drake*

Enos
> (EE-NOS)
> Ex: *Enos Sartin Tale*

Ensley
> Ex: *Jill Ensley Winter*

Eola
> (EE-O-LA)
> Ex: *Eola Wikes*

Eoline
>Ex: *Sally Eoline Baker*

Ephraim
>Ex: *Ephraim Sayad*

Erasmus
>Ex: *Erasmus Clones*

Erte
>Ex: *Melissa Erte Cannes*

Escalon
>Ex: *Escalon Cayanos Seville*

Escondido
>Ex: *Escondido Jay*

Escovedo
>Ex: *Escovedo Valdine Ramiriz*

Esenel
>Ex: *Esenel Beckler Highland*

Essena
>Ex: *Essena Williams Sen*

Esseno
>(ESS-EE-NO)
>Ex: *Esseno Serrina Haywood*

Estero
>Ex: *Estero Grant Lorrento*

Etzel
>Ex: *Hillary Etzel Hayes*

Eubie
>(U-BEE)
>Ex: *Eubie Reeds*

Euclid
>Ex: *Euclid Cintra Sashton*

Euenar
>(YOU-N-R)
>Ex: *Euenar Petrash*

Eulalia
>(OO-LAY-LEE-AH)
>Ex: *Eulalia Carey*

Evora
> (EV-OR-AH or EE-VOR-AH)
> Ex: *Evora Marie Genetti Bautista*

Fax
> Ex: *Fax Carrington*

Fellini
> Ex: *Base Fellini Jackonetti*

Fenton
> Ex: *Fenton Keller*

Fidelma
> Ex: *Fidelma May*

Fidora
> Ex: *Fidora Stallone*

Filbert
> Ex: *Filbert Paston*

Fillmore
> Ex: *Amy Fillmore Bransford*

Filly
> Ex: *Filly Wheaton Sulikowski*

Fimo
> Ex: *Fimo Raites*

Finley
> Ex: *Finley Sarah Smith*

Finnial
> Ex: *Jacqueline Finnial Sanns*

Fire
> Ex: *Fire Richo Roberts*

Fisbie
> Ex: *Fisbie Jill Anniston*

Fisher
> Ex: *Fisher Kayler Brown*

Flash
> Ex: *Flash Phelps*

Flicka
> Ex: *Flicka Alexa Peralta Maria McGurrin*

Flinn
Ex: *Flinn Martine Perrinson*
Flint
Ex: *Flint Fredricks*
Flip
Ex: *Flip Johnson Jones*
Florinda
Ex: *Florinda Maria Corrina Fuentes*
Flynt
Ex: *Flynt Axton*
Foley
Ex: *Foley Maxton Freeland*
Folsom
Ex: *Folsom Baker Howes*
Fontana
Ex: *Fontana Greene*
Formica
Ex: *Formica Dinette*
Forsythe
Ex: *Carlson Forsythe Santini*
Fossil
Ex: *Jackson Fossil Dred*
Froujke
(FROWK)
Ex: *Melissa Froujke Abbott*
Fulton
Ex: *Sara Fulton Mendelcraton*

Gadget
Ex: *Michael Gadget David*
Gaenor
Ex: *Gaenor Wake Merrins*
Galena
Ex: *Galena Carlotta Sorento*
Gannett
Ex: *Jerrund Gannett Torrintale*
Gaton
Ex: *Gaton Barry Trikes*
Gaugin
Ex: *Texler Gaugin Stevens*
Gavlin
Ex: *Gavlin Martin Sperry*
Geary
Ex: *Geary Walton Goldstine*
Gekko
Ex: *Gekko Brakes*

Geneva
Ex: *Geneva Betty Riche*
Geo
Ex: *Geo Jorland Giles*
Gero
(JARE-O)
Ex: *Gero Martinez Blake*
Gershwin
Ex: *Gershwin Batin Moore*
Gimo
Ex: *Gimo Perrini*
Gin
Ex: *Gin Thomas*
Ginseng
Ex: *Ginseng Sara Ellsworth*
Godiva
Ex: *Godiva Bright*
Gold
Ex: *Jack Gold Rain*

Goleta

Ex: *Cindy Goleta Tinstow*

Gotham

Ex: *Gotham Mary Erikson*

Grain

Ex: *Grain Bill Miles*

Grandcanyon

Ex: *Lucille Grandcanyon Porter*

Green

Ex: *Green Teakes*

Grenada

Ex: *Grenada Prascilla Cortnella*

Griffin

Ex: *Griffin Sikes*

Grinnel

Ex: *Sylvia Grinnel Marin*

Guage

Ex: *Guage Willis Rhork*

Guatemala

Ex: *Sussana Guatemala Cerres*

Guaymas

Ex: *Guaymas Ellen Winston*

Guilder

Ex: *Guilder Lane Rhodes*

Guilin

Ex: *Guilin Saxby Price*

Gunn

Ex: *Gunn Lewis Steer*

Haasel
> (HA-SULL)
> Ex: *Haasel Jordan Paytes*

Hale
> Ex: *J Hale Jones*

Halifax
> Ex: *Samuel Halifax Baxter*

Halloway
> Ex: *Halloway Cobalt Shores*

Halogen
> Ex: *Halogen Lindsey Sands*

Halon
> Ex: *Halon Gregory Rings*

Hanover
> Ex: *Manny Hanover Rubenstein*

Harlem
> Ex: *Harlem Lucy Strikes*

Harmon
> Ex: *Harmon Lenny Sills*

Haromi
> (HARE-O-ME)
> Ex: *Marissa Haromi Jentzen*

Harrell
> Ex: *Harrell Roland Rey*

Harumi
> (HA-ROO-ME)
> Ex: *Jules Harumi Johnston*

Harvard
> Ex: *Harvard Stone*

Havana
> Ex: *Havana Marie Sartaynja*

Hayden
> Ex: *Hayden Wells*

Hayes
> Ex: *Hayes Brinell Sares*

Haylo
> Ex: *Felicia Haylo Vintercourt*

Hayworth
>Ex: *Hayworth Rachel Llord*

Hazelton
>Ex: *Perry Hazelton Phillips*

Hazen
>Ex: *Hazen Jacqueline Saints*

Hemlock
>Ex: *Clorissa Hemlock Rands*

Hennesey
>Ex: *Hennesey C White*

Hepsebaugh
>Ex: *Hepsebaugh Harlan Spivey*

Heron
>Ex: *Heron Aston Kales*

Heusen
>Ex: *Robert Heusen Storlan*

Hiero
>(HE-AIR-OH)
>Ex: *Jacques Hiero Linnson*

Highland
>Ex: *Bobby Highland Black*

Hiko
>(HE-KO)
>Ex: *Hiko Ditto Dayes*

Hilo
>Ex: *Hilo Bento Takano*

Hilton
>Ex: *Hilton James Heuer*

Hemmingway
>Ex: *Eldridge Hemmingway Ryemore*

Hine
>Ex: *Hine Lester Loomis*

Hockney
>Ex: *Gerrund Hockney Jones*

Hollywood
>Ex: *Hollywood Sam Stelleri*

H

Hopkins
> Ex: *Hopkins Toland Dex*

Howlin
> Ex: *Perrin Howlin Lanlon*

Huxley
> Ex: *Huxley Tennor Rainnin*

Hyatt
> Ex: *Hyatt Latton Drake*

Hyde
> Ex: *Hyde Willis Laton*

Hydro
> Ex: *Hydro Piedmont Pakes*

I
> Ex: *I Corlin Tynan*

Iaco
> (EE-AH-KO)
> Ex: *Iaco Green Satayno*

Iakora
> (EE-AH-KOR-AH)
> Ex: *Iakora Lynn Korani*

Ichino
> (IH-KEY-NO)
> Ex: *Ichino Moro Kobin*

Idol
> Ex: *Idol West*

Idoya
> (EE-DOY-UH)
> Ex: *Idoya Corrine Bess*

Iko
> (EE-KO)
> Ex: *Iko Theresa Norkandinsko*

Ilex
> Ex: *Ilex Black*

Illa
> Ex: *Illa Vicenza Sorrena*

Illinois
> Ex: *Illinois Stevens*

Imo
> Ex: *Imo Ricks*

Imogen
> Ex: *Julyn Imogen Kate*

Impala
> Ex: *Roquel Imapala Moore*

Inc
> Ex: *Inc Sands*

Indiana
> Ex: *Indiana Tappin Roads*

Indigo
> Ex: *Indigo Jane Wethers*

Indo
>   Ex: *Indo Lowpin Becks*

Indra
>   Ex: *Sara Indra Fines*

Inglewood
>   Ex: *Inglewood Baxter Weslyn*

Ingo
>   Ex: *Ingo Rice*

Iolo
>   Ex: *Iolo Charlin Torrine*

Iona
>   Ex: *Iona Phillips*

Ionica
>   Ex: *Ionica Vaness Dietz*

Iora
>   (EE-OR-UH)
>   Ex: *Iora Rainey Mae*

Iota
>   Ex: *David Iota Juleston*

Iowa
>   Ex: *Jennifer Iowa Banks*

Ipso
>   Ex: *Ipso Noland Dorkanski*

Ireland
>   Ex: *Chet Ireland Chase*

Iro
>   Ex: *Sperry Iro Packard*

Irvine
>   Ex: *Jaqueline Irvine West*

Ishin
>   Ex: *Sidney Ishin Lee*

Isiolo
>   (I-CEE-O-LOW)
>   Ex: *Isiolo Kay Tano*

Island
>   Ex: *Jenny Island Saints*

Isle

Ex: *John Isle Rainin*

Isola

Ex: *Isola Crae*

Ives

Ex: *Bateman Ives Lyndenson*

Ivory

Ex: *Jorlin Ivory Cates*

Izzy

Ex: *Izzy Fenns*

Jaakko
>(JAY-KO)
>Ex: *Jaakko C Rappaport*

Jacaro
>Ex: *Jacaro J London*

Jaeger
>(YEA-GER)
>Ex: *Jaeger T Ollander*

Jag
>Ex: *Jag J Tekkor*

Jaice
>Ex: *Jaice Stevens*

Jakarta
>Ex: *Jakarta Black*

Jalon
>Ex: *Jalon Perry Smith*

Jamaica
>Ex: *Jamaica Earl Jones*

Jamal
>Ex: *Jamal Even Saintes*

Janneau
>(JAN-O)
>Ex: *Julie Janneau West*

Javanese
>Ex: *Javanese Ojeda*

Jayena
>Ex: *Ruby Jaena Bates*

Jayenel
>Ex: *Jayenel C Rollins*

Jenkins
>Ex: *Jenkins Steele*

Jergen
>Ex: *Jergen Aston Borrenskovitch*

Jerico
>Ex: *Jerico Jaime Sorrenton*

Jerilyn
>Ex: *Jerilyn B Maxton*

Jersey
    Ex: *Jersey Shores*
Jetson
    Ex: *Jetson Khorin Dodson*
Jetta
    Ex: *Jetta Leslie Gonsalez*
Jetty
    Ex: *Jetty Krausen*
Jeust
    Ex: *Jeust Morena*
Jimno
    Ex: *Jimno Montgomery*
Jinx
    Jinx Carmen Corona
Jitzu
    Ex: *Jitzu Imura Icardo*
Jixi
    Ex: *Jixi Marshine*
Jovan
    (YO-VAUGHN)
    Ex: *Jovan Satner Solkantovich*
Josefa
    Ex: *Josefa Farine Tulare*
Jucara
    Ex: *Jucara Victor Monrovio*
Juneau
    Ex: *Juneau Sarmiento Rontino*
Jungle
    Ex: *Sumara Jungle Mirantes*
Juniper
    Ex: *Juniper Jade Rellina*
Justice
    Ex: *Milton Justice Sadler*
Jute
    Ex: *Jute Clifford McCutcheon*

Kaanapali
   Ex: *Kaanapali Lea Loa*
Kahlo
   Ex: *Kahlo Dalo McCrea*
Kaiser
   Ex: *Kaiser McDonald*
Kalana
   Ex: *Kalana Rena Ferrara*
Kale
   Ex: *Kale T Wexford*
Kandinsky
   Ex: *Rich Kandinsky Fischman*
Kane
   Ex: *Kane Angela Ferrintino*
Kansas
   Ex: *Kansas Cantor Fikes*
Karastan
   Ex: *Karastan Roselyn Golde*
Kardel
   Ex: *Kardel Griffen Jefferson*
Karim
   Ex: *Salana Karim Jutowski*
Kavel
   Ex: *Kavel Arron Kirtland*
Kayak
   Ex: *Kayak Kristin Klassen*
Kayhan
   Ex: *Kayhan Ghodsi*

Keemun
   Ex: *Keemun Cane Sasnish*
Keena
   Ex: *Keena Teresa McKinley*
Kegan
   Ex: *Kegan McDougald*
Keiko
   (KAY-KO)
   Ex: *Keiko Jul Skate*

Kellog
  Ex: *Kellog Roger Coates*
Kellyn
  Ex: *Kellyn Besty Rhodin*
Kelso
  Ex: *Kelso Ashton Price*
Kendall
  Ex: *Kendall Jay Bexler*
Kendra
  Ex: *Kendra Hanna Smith*
Keno
  Ex: *Keno Jack Sultanin*
Kenova
  Ex: *Kenova Reena Tales*
Kenyon
  Ex: *Kenyon Rales*
Keoka
  Ex: *Keoka Sato Argabright*
Keoki
  Ex: *Keoki C Terrako*
Keoko
  Ex: *Keoko Michelle Catterson*
Kerouac
  Ex: *Kerouac Alderman*
Kestrel
  Ex: *Meagan Kestrel Bharnes*
Keswick
  Ex: *Keswick J Satchfeld*
Kevlin
  Ex: *Kevlin Mars*
Kiliminjaro
  Ex: *Chistopher Kiliminjaro Jonns*
Kilo
  Ex: *Kilo Venlin*
Kilty
  Ex: *Samson Kilty Kales*

Kincaid

Ex: *Kincaid Rhode*

Kingston

Ex: *Gerome Kingston Nicholes*

Kiosk

Ex; Kiosk Banes

Kiowa

Ex: *Kiowa Bonnie Bates*

Kirala

Ex: *Kirala Jane Roberts*

Kirin

Ex: *Kirin Decca Brades*

Kitano

Ex: *Kitano Wattes*

Klee

Ex: *Klee Whitten Dorrin*

Knight

Ex: *Knight Reed*

Knota

(NOTE-UH)

Ex: *Knota Steel Rites*

Knox

Ex: *Wilson Knox Bailerton*

Koala

Ex: *Koala Richtes*

Kobe

Ex: *Kobe Lei Pare*

Kodiak

Ex: *Kodiak Bankington*

Kohler

Ex: *Kohler C Winston*

Kojak

Ex: *Kojak Jerrund Morrris*

Kona

Ex: *Kona Liani Layna*

Koria

Ex: *Koria Lassin*

Kyburz
    Ex: *Kyburz Teakin Rast*

La Paz
> Ex: *La Paz Holland*

Laakin
> (LA-KIN)
> Ex: *Laakin Jarra Lincot*

Laykin
> Ex: *Laykin Khares*

Lafayette
> Ex: *Layfayette Lewis*

Landon
> Ex: *Landon T Sparks*

Lapis
> Ex: *Lapis Jace Stol*

Laredo
> Ex: *John Laredo Settby*

Lariat
> Ex: *Lariat William Finee*

Larissa
> Ex: *Larissa Langston Farr*

Larkin
> Ex: *Larkin Pratmore*

Larkspur
> Ex: *Larkspur Cheryl Rites*

Lasher
> Ex: *Lasher Marx*

Lassen
> Ex: *Lassen C Courts*

Latch
> Ex: *Latch Polin*

Lausanne
> Ex: *Lausanne Sorenna*

Lavell
> Ex: *Lavell Lakeston*

Lawton
> Ex: *Lawton John Coneston*

Lela
> Ex: *Lelongoa Alexa Levi*

Lennox
>   Ex: *Lisa Lennox Grace*

Leota
>   Ex: *Leota Jale Scorson*

Levon
>   Ex: *Levon Miles*

Lexine
>   Ex: *Lixine Milly Landon*

Lilac
>   Ex: *Lilac Mazy Moss*

Linc
>   Ex: *Linc Morgan*

Linden
>   Ex: *Linden P Argyle*

Lindo
>   Ex: *Lindo Rondelli*

Linfield
>   Ex: *Linfield Lawson*

Linnet
>   Ex: *Torrin Linnet Taylin*

Linwood
>   Ex: *Linwood Rocksford*

Lirion
>   Ex: *Jules Lirion Jacket*

Lixi
>   Ex: *Lixi Dobri*

Lodi
>   (LOW-DYE)
>   Ex: *Lodi Walker*

London
>   Ex: *Lauren London Waytes*

Lortel
>   Ex: *Lortel Dorensko*

Lotus
>   Ex: *Lotus Lee Paxford*

Lovejoy
>   Ex: *Julia Lovejoy Sibbet*

L

Lowell
Ex: *Lowell Dorin Toland*
Loyola
Ex: *Loyola Sills Westford*
Lozanos
Ex: *Lozanos Corone Sabin*
Lucerne
Ex: *Lucerne T Rexor*
Lucia
Ex: *Lucia Marie Ginetti*
Luminere
Ex: *Noreen Luminere Billing*
Lupine
Ex: *Michael Lupine Blades*
Luxe
Ex: *Luxe Bocarski*
Lynden
Ex: *Lynden Stiles*
Lyndon
Ex: *Lydon Paris*
Lyne
Ex: *Lyne Marcus Rand*
Lynford
Ex: *Lynford Price*
Lynon
Ex: *Lynon Karen Tones*
Lynx
Ex: *Lynx Setlin*
Lyra
Ex: *Lyra Karmine*

L

Masai

(MA-SIGH)

Ex: *Masai C Catttamar*

Macado

Ex: *Macado Crae*

Macay

Ex: *Macay Foster*

Madeira

Ex: *Luchesa Madeira Ronneta*

Madox

Ex: *Lisa Madox Danielson*

Madras

Ex: *Jacqueline Madras Bellingcourt*

Madrid

Ex: *Madrid Sienna Sakes*

Maduro

Ex: *Julian Maduro Grants*

Magenta

Ex: *Magenta Rose*

Magnolia

Ex: *Magnolia Lucy Marrington*

Maiko

Ex: *Maiko Connor Stennmar*

Maine

Ex: *Maine Jenner Straits*

Mairobi

Ex: *Jules Mairobi Braxtin*

Majave

(MA-YA-VEE)

Ex: Ex: *Majave Rachel Banes*

Maki

(MA-KEY)

Ex: *Maki West Tobenta*

Malachite

Ex: *Malachite Hale*

Malaza

Ex: *Rolin Malaza Spade*

Malden

Ex: *Malden Dean Sonderville*

Maletti

Ex: *Susan Maletti Barrett*

Mallorca

(MY-OR-CA)

Ex: *Mallorca Maria Vanettto*

Malone

Ex: *Malone Stevens*

Malta

Ex: *Malta C Corlanetti*

Mandarin

Ex: *Corinna Mandarin DuPont*

Manet

(MAA-NAY)

Ex: *Senna Manet Pascal*

Manx

Ex: *Benjamin Manx Dolland*

Marden

Ex: *Marden Cannor Tillmans*

Marengo

Ex: *Marengo Colant Seremo*

Margolin

Ex: *Margolin Ballantynne*

Marigolde

Ex: *Marigolde Delgado*

Marijke

(MARE-I-KA)

Ex: *Marijke Terpstra*

Marimba

Ex: *Susanne Marimba Felice*

Marina

Ex: *Marina Rachelle Delano*

Mariner

Ex: *Islo Mariner Esposito*

Mariposa
    Ex: *Mariposa Leah Freedlund*
Marisol
    Ex: *Marisol Julis Gantt*
Marlin
    Ex: *Marlin Garcia Goldstein*
Marlon
    Ex: *Marlon Henrik Cartsworth*
Marmac
    Ex: *Marmac Jackson Cates*
Maronnet
    Ex: *Marronet Hayden*
Marsala
    Ex: *Marsala Hatheway*
Martell
    Ex: *Martell T Sicado*
Martini
    Ex: *Martini West*
Marwan
    Ex: *Marwan Noel Sabbagh*
Mash
    Ex: *Wexford Mash Trains*
Masonic
    Ex: *Masonic Post*
Match
    Ex: *Match T Mason*
Mateo
    Ex: *Mateo Sortinella*
Matisse
    Ex: *Matisse Berrin Jenni*
Maytag
    Ex: *Maytag Corin Blue*
McAllister
    Ex: *McAllister Payne Webster*
McBey
    Ex: *McBey Darwin Woods*

McCall

Ex: *McCall Torrence Willks*

McGraw

Ex: *McGraw Heath*

McGurrin

Ex: *McGurrin Seton Leibert*

McRae

Ex: *McRae Ashlin Stockard*

Mecca

Ex: *Mecca Miles Price*

Medanos

Ex: *Rachel Medanos Mendoza*

Medina

Ex: *Medina Ray Rolands*

Meighan

(MEE-IN)

Ex: *Meighan Williams Leibert*

Melbourne

Ex: *Luci Melbourne Arrows*

Melton

Ex: *Melton Davis*

Memphis

Ex: *Itore Memphis Sottsass*

Menakhaya

(MEN-UH-KIE-UH)

Ex: *Kenna Menakhaya Raines*

Mendel

Ex: *Mendel Jackson*

Mendocino

Ex: *Mendocino Parker*

Mercury

Ex: *Roland Mercury Rohe*

Merdoc

Ex: *Merdoc Jeffery Payne*

Meridien

Ex: *Meridien Tamara Grove*

Merino

Ex: *Merino T Venturo*

Mero

(MARE-O)

Ex: *Mero Siquedo Dungala*

Merrimac

Ex: *Merrimac Scherer*

Mesa

Ex: *Mesa Zona*

Metro

Ex: *Metro Baxter*

Mexico

Ex: *Mexico Santo Viera*

Michigan

Ex: *David Michigan Lockwood*

Mieno

(ME-AY-NO)

Ex: *Mieno Kay Tokin*

Miilo

(MY-LOW)

Ex: *Miilo Roberts*

Mikado

(ME-KA-DO)

Ex: *Mikado Yoshi Corolla*

Mikkelson

Ex: *Jack Mikkelson Dice*

Millenium

Ex: *Maron Millenium Mitchells*

Million

Ex: *Million Stolinovitchcoff*

Mimosa

Ex: *Mimosa Maria Martell*

Minda

Ex: *Minda McDaniels*

Ming

Ex: *Julie Ming Schwarts*

Mingo
> Ex: *Mingo Nakano*

Minnow
> Ex: *Minnow Parkington*

Minorca
> Ex: *Minorca Ruby*

Minta
> Ex: *Minta Manx*

Minthe
> Ex: *Minthe Alice Dine*

Mirada
> Ex: *Mirada Ferrari*

Mirinda
> Ex: *Mirinda Costa Mira*

Miro
> (MERE-OH)
> Ex: *Nichol Miro Gianni*

Missoula
> Ex: *Missoula Roquelle Montana*

Missouri
> Ex: *Braemar Missouri Jacobs*

Miyako
> Ex: *Miyako Kaytano*

Mizner
> Ex: *Mizner Ritchell Jones*

Mobil
> Ex: *Mobil SonderOrtinez*

Mobile
> Ex: *Mobile Sari Osmani*

Mobius
> Ex: *Mobius Kates*

Modena
> Ex: *Modena Ayla Sorrento*

Mojave
> Ex: *Kaydo Mojave Brit*

Molina
> Ex: *Molina Maria Maretti*

Monaco
Ex: *Monaco Angela Mida*
Monet
(MO-NAY)
Ex: *Monet Jina Latin*
Money
Ex: *Jackson Money Takks*
Monopole
Ex: *Reann Monopole Burlynn*
Monroe
Ex: *Monroe Stennson*
Montague
(MON-TA-GIEW)
Ex: *Montague Jase*
Montana
Ex: *Montana Jameson Larussa*
Montego
Ex: *Lawernce Montego Venetto*
Montgomery
Ex: *Eldon Montgomery Blues*
Montrose
Ex: *Montrose West*
Moreno
Ex: *Serrin Moreno Caines*
Morro
Ex: *Constance Morro Lattin*
Mortise
Ex: *Mortise Laskin Fornello*
Mosaic
Ex: *Mosaic T Osorino*
Moscow
Ex: *Lorraine Moscow Antonia*
Mosson
(MO-SON)
Ex: *Mosson Tory Martinez*

Mota

(MO-TAH)

Ex: *Mota James*

Moxie

Ex: *Moxie Perrin Miotel*

Muana Loa

Ex: *Muana Loa Iles*

Muller

(MIU-LER)

Ex: *Muller Giordan Rebbel*

Mvolo

Ex: *Mvolo Rex Rientos*

Myo

Ex: *Myo Goldstein*

Myorca

Ex: *Myorca Yoskiko Tallavera*

Myrh

(MURR)

Ex: *Dusty Myrh Blone*

Nashville
     Ex: *Susan Nashville Hartlin*
Namerology
     Ex: *Namerology Praxton Price*
Nandina
     Ex: *Nandina T Sparks*
Nanimo
     Ex: *Nanimo Pettiman*
Narsai
     (NAR-CEE)
     Narsai Michael David
Nari
     Ex: *Michelle Nari Abbott*
Nasa
     Ex: *Nasa Warren Tackin*
Nash
     Ex: *Nash Wailin Greenes*
Nashville
     Ex: *Nashville Cats*
Nato
     Ex: *Nato Sorren Grove*
Natoma
     Ex: *Natoma Rocken State*
Nautica
     Ex: *Sally Nautica Holland*
Navak
     Ex: *Navak Pond*
Navy
     Ex: *Navy Connor Jannets*
Neo
      Ex: *Neo Macintosh*
Neon
     Ex: *Neon Charles Whitfield*
Neptune
     Ex: *Celestine Neptune Sands*
Nero
     Ex: *Nero Graham*

Nether
> Ex: *Nether Hollander*

Nevin
> Ex: *Nivin Place*

Newport
> Ex: *Newport Seymore Glickstein*

Nico
> Ex: *Nico Cartwright*

Nido
> Ex: *Nido Dakin Rappacourt*

Nightingale
> Ex: *Nightingale Deena Agellin*

Nikel
> Ex: *Nikel Blanes*

Nile
> Ex: *Nile Steve Witherton*

Niro
> Ex: *Niro Stone*

Nitro
> Ex: *Nitro Glass Storler*

Nonce
> Ex: *Nonce Pera Valdeen*

Norrell
> Ex: *Maureen Norrell Blackes*

Noveau
> (NO-VO)
> Ex: *Noveau Charlin Nemin*

Novena
> (NO-VEH-NUH or NO-VEE-NA)
> Ex: *Novena Mari Solento*

O
    Ex: *O Rona Coran*
Obit
    Ex: *Obit T Jones*
Odeon
    Ex: *Odeon Ryan Wilson*

Odessa
    Ex: *Odessa Jana Erikson*
Odin
    Ex: *Odin C Tollin*
Oeno
    (O-AY-NO)
    Ex: *Oeno Kaylin Lewis*
Ohana
    Ex: *Ohana Bixland*
Ohai
    (O-HIGH)
    Ex: *Ohai Matson*
Ohio
    Ex: *Ohio Barrents*
Oka
    Ex: *Oka Shares*
O'keefe
    Ex: *O'keefe Perrins Stonnings*
Ola
    Ex: *Ola Ferrindo*
Olin
    Ex: *Olin C Ferrari*
Olinda
    Ex: *Olinda Dashmar*
Olive
    Ex: *Olive Terrin Boyanowski*
Omaha
    Ex: *Omaha Makler Brinnelsson*
Oman
    Ex: *Oman Wastin Carrington*

Omega
   Ex: *Omega Benin Garristore*
Omer
   Ex: *Omer Clayes Fellinton*
Ooloo
   (EW-LOO)
   Ex: *Ooloo Emily Waldron*
Opal
   Ex: *Opal Sella Hendrickson*
Oram
   Ex: *Oram Pine Clares*
Orbit
   Ex: *Orbit Stells*
Orchid
   Ex: *Rainey Orchid Dyne*
Oreana
   (O-REE-NA)
   Ex: *Oreana Annie Bates*
Orilla
   Ex: *Orilla Linda Vienos*
Orinda
   Ex: *Orinda Day Ilanda*
Oriole
   Ex: *Oriole Stevens*
Orion
   Ex: *Orion Bateson*
Oro
   Ex: *Oro C Mendelsen*
Orrin
   Ex: *Orrin Craston Flips*
Orsi
   Ex: *Franklin Orsi Lauder*
Ortez
   Ex: *Ortez Manuel Carracas*
Orvieto
   Ex: *Orvieto Jones*

Orwell
    Ex: *Orwell Briscoe*
Osaka
    Ex: *Osaka Isakuro*
Osborne
    Ex: *Cheryl Osborne Sanson*
Osetra
    Ex: *Jenna Osetra Francisco*
Osla
    Ex: *Osla Irvine Iscane*
Oslo
    Ex: *Oslo C Robbins*
Oster
    Ex: *Oster Cates*
Otaki
    Ex: *Otaki Elliko*
Ouzo
    (OO-ZO)
    Ex: *Ouzo Berrin Skolkavinoski*
Ovieda
    Ex: *Ovieda Maria Taranella*
Oviedo
    Ex: *Oviedo Braxton Post*
Oyal
    (OIL)
    Ex: *Oyal Saze Alliston*
Oz
    Ex: *Oz Layton Janes*
Ozark
    Ex: *Sam Ozark Ilands*

Pace
> Ex: *Pace Saunders*

Pacific
> Ex: *Willis Pacific Price*

Pacifica
> Ex: *Pacifica Dino*

Palatino
> Ex: *Palatino Emma Plattes*

Pali
> Ex: *Pali Daston*

Panama
> Ex: *Panama Sails Fellini*

Panna
> Ex: *Panna Cotta Jone*

Para
> Ex: *Para Torrin Tales*

Parade
> Ex: *Parade Orlin Mollison*

Paradise
> Ex: *Anne Paradise Larsen*

Paradiso
> Ex: *Paradiso Pettano*

Paramount
> Ex: *Paramount Christo Revine*

Parish
> Ex: *Maxwell Parish Dores*

Parson
> Ex: *Parson Phillips*

Pasha
> Ex: *Lauranne Pasha Verra*

Pasqua
> Ex: *Pasqua Kara Tates*

Patina
> Ex: *Jaqueline Patina Rave*

Patton
> Ex: *Patton Price*

Pendleton
>Ex: *Pendleton Billington*

Pendula
>Ex: *Pendula Rachele Wells*

Pennsylvania
>Ex: *Pennsylvania C Tycour*

Peralta
>Ex: *Peralta Meris Deins*

Perdido
>Ex: *Perdido Durango*

Peridot
>Ex: *Peridot Yorinsin*

Perrin
>Ex: *Perrin Miles*

Peru
>Ex: *Bilden Peru Berrin*

Peetes
>Ex: *Peetes Wexford*

Petcoff
>Ex: *Martin Petcoff Renneski*

Peugeot
>(PU-ZJO)
>Ex: *Peugeot Spassovski*

Peyton
>Ex: *Peyton Rexford*

Phantom
>Ex: *Phontom Cains*

Phelps
>Ex: *Phelps Norrins*

Philadelphia
>Ex: *Philadelphia Parrington*

Phoenix
>Ex: *Phoenix Rhodes*

Pico
>Ex: *Pico Arroyo*

Piedmont
>Ex: *Piedmont Royals*

Pierino
>(P-AIR-EE-NO)
>Ex: *Pierino Venalta*

Pierot
>(P-AIR-OH)
>Ex: *Pierot Salvaggio*

Pilot
>Ex: *Pilot Morriston*

Pilsner
>Ex: *Sayna Pilsner Waynes*

Pitney
>Ex: *Pitney O Thomasson*

Pixel
>Ex: *Pixel Anne Ryerson*

Pixi
>Ex: *Pixi Staten*

Poet
>Ex: *Poet Sites*

Poland
>Ex: *Jori Poland Dayland*

Polaris
>Ex: *Polaris Robbins*

Pomona
>Ex: *Lee Pomona Giffen*

Porter
>Ex: *Porter Saxby*

Powell
>Ex: *Powell Johnson*

Presidio
>Ex: *Presidio Fites*

Price
>Ex: *Price T Walkin*

Quaid
   Ex: *Quaid Chex*
Quebec
   Ex: *Quebec Stevens*
Quill
   Ex: *Quill Fenter Stapleton*
Quillin
   Ex: *Quillin Jerrund Jossens*
Quimby
   Ex: *Quimby Allton*
Quince
   Ex: *Gilda Quince Bayes*
Quinley
   Ex: *Quinley Scott*

Radcliff
Ex: *Radcliff Sites*
Rada
Ex: *Rada Petcoff*
Rado
(REY-DO or RAH-DO)
Ex: *Rado Lisson Reeds*
Rainer
Ex: *Rainer Janes*
Raines
Ex: *Raines Peyton Seyerton*
Ralland
Ex: *Ralland Smith*

Ralston
Ex: *Ralston Terrence Cartwrighte*
Ramero
Ex: *Ramero Bettes*
Ramic
Ex: *Ramic Lewis Lynden*
Ramos
Ex: *Ramos Vennin*
Rand
Ex: *Rand Lock Shorelands*
Rapallo
Ex: *Rapallo Bose Nealand*
Rasina
Ex: *Rasina Carrie Sattsworth*
Raskin
Ex: *Raskin Jones*
Raven
Ex: *Raven Marston*
Raydon
Ex: *Raydon Poland Rexler*
Raymar
Ex: *Raymar Feinland*
Red
Ex: *Red Jacks*

Reeves

Ex: *Reeves Kallington*

Regatta

Ex: *Regatta Shelton*

Regent

Ex: *Regent T Moore*

Reidel

(RYE-DELL)

Ex: *Reidel Wakesfield*

Reiland

(RYE-LAND)

Ex: *Reiland Pakkerton*

Rembrandt

Ex: *Rembrandt T Skolanski*

Renida

Ex: *Renida Dakston*

Renoir

Ex: *Renoir Sira Annato*

Renwick

Ex: *Renwick Larkin Casselmar*

Reuse

Ex: *Reuse Baxton*

Revelle

Ex: *Revelle Nera Hennestan*

Reynard

Ex: *Reynard Phillips*

Reznor

Ex: *Reznor Tolland Wellston*

Rhen

Ex: *Leena Rhen Rittsmer*

Rhode

Ex: *Rhode Kellerin*

Rhodes

Ex: *Julan Rhodes Schaler*

Rhone

Ex: *Rhone Stein*

Rialta
>Ex: *Rialta Rose Pirella*

Rialto
>Ex: *Rialto Dino Tellani*

Riata
>(REE-AH-TA)
>Ex: *Riata Sena Merrina*

Rice
>Ex: *Rice Tyemore Cains*

Richmond
>Ex: *Richmond Davis*

Richter
>(RICK-TER)
>Ex: *Richter Ballanski*

Ridley
>Ex: *Ridley Sakes*

Rio
>Ex: *Rio Corrado*

Ritz
>Ex: *Denna Ritz Westmar*

Riven
>Ex: *Riven Kyle Lirassen*

Rivet
>Ex: *Rivet Jakes*

Riyal
>Ex: *Riyal T Hane*

Robe
>Ex: *Robe Bronstin*

Roble
>Ex: *Roble T Raddisen*

Rock
>Ex: *Rock Milton Edisson*

Rodeo
>Ex: *Layton Rodeo Jayez*

Rodin
>Ex: *Rodin Sikes*

Roleen
>   Ex: *Roleen Mirando Cortez*

Romain
>   Ex: *Julan Romain Merris*

Rondo
>   Ex: *Rondo Consello*

Ronin
>   Ex: *Ronin Charton*

Rousseau
>   Ex: *Rousseau Gaston Morrai*

Royce
>   Ex: *Royce Silverton*

Rubicon
>   Ex: *Rubicon Francisco*

Rubine
>   Ex: *Rubine Rose*

Ruellia
>   (ROO-EL-EE-UH)
>   Ex: *Ruellia Marie Sallina*

Rupi
>   Ex: *Rupi Sans*

Safari
　　Ex: *Safari Lange*
Safford
　　Ex: *Safford Tye Price*
Saffron
　　Ex: *Saffron Julie Lestin*
Sage
　　Ex: *Sage Price*
Sahara
　　Ex: *Sahara Dray*
Sail
　　Ex: *Sail Milts*
Sailes
　　Ex: *Sailes Lisa Daye*
Sake
　　Ex: *Sake Terrison*

Saks
　　Ex: *Mary Saks Westin*
Salem
　　Ex: *Salem Shores*
Salen
　　Ex: *Salen Eldo Torres*
Salinger
　　Ex: *Salinger Greene*
Salt
　　Ex: *Salt Jeffsen*
Samir
　　Ex: *Samir Shabilla*
Sansome
　　Ex: *Sansome J Foxner*
Santana
　　Ex: *Santana Domingo Vortenya*
Sapphire
　　Ex: *Katherine Sapphire Si*
Saran
　　Ex: *Saran Marie Deltano*

Saroyan
Ex: *Saroyan Korani*
Sash
Ex: *Sash Lucky Cares*
Sashiko
Ex: *Susan Sashiko Lee*
Saskia
Ex: *Caroline Saskia Abbott*
Sato
(SAY-TOW)
Ex: *Sato Cales Yoshinto*
Sattelite
Ex: *Sattelite Jino Vallentes*
Sattler
Ex: *Rick Sattler Sonnes*
Saurus
Ex: *Saurus Trekk*
Sauterne
Ex: *Sauterne Reyna Palis*
Savin
Ex: *Savin Anis Lira*
Savoy
Ex: *Savoy Rites*
Saxby
Ex: *Saxby West*
Sayre
Ex: *Sayre T Jal*
Schale
Ex: *Schale Kares*
Schell
Ex: *Laura Schell Wallace*
Scorsese
(SCORE-SAY-CEE)
Ex: *James Scorsese Ballacondi*
Scotch
Ex: *Scotch Braxton*

Seaford
 Ex: *Seaford Miles Vellis*
Seal
 Ex: *Rilford Seal Cansoen*
Seales
 Ex: *Seales Jorr*
Seastar
 Ex: *Vic Seastar Windes*
Sedona
 Ex: *Sam Sedona Prattes*
Seeno
 (C-NO)
 Ex: *Seeno Mani Santorino*
Segal
 Ex: *Segal Grace*
Segovia
 Ex: *Roland Segovia Garcia*

Seiler
 (SAY-LER)
 Ex: *Seiler North*
Seketo
 (SEH-KAY-TOW)
 Ex: *Seketo Nakaru*
Selena
 (SEL-AY-NA)
 Ex: *Selena Ile Cantore*
Sella
 Ex: *Sella Starlin*
Selton
 Ex: *Richard Selton Giles*
Selva
 Ex: *Selva Smith*
Selvet
 Ex: *Selvet Maria Stares*
Seneca
 Ex: *Seneca J Williams*

Sential
>Ex: *Sential Mary Ferante*

Sephora
>Ex: *Sephora Marcia Wills*

Seravando
>Ex: *Seravando Costillando*

Serenade
>Ex: *Serenade Bastille*

Serin
>Ex: *Serin O Wilkens*

Serrano
>Ex: *Serrano Callinda*

Serre
>Ex: *Serre Talikovsky*

Serrena
>Ex: *Serrena Quelannos*

Serrone
>Ex: *Serrone Jarin Fellini*

Sesoto
>Ex: *Sesoto Ellyn Brochair*

Seton
>(CEE-TON)
>Ex: *Seton Vaines*

Seuss
>Ex: *Carlo Seuss Dexler*

Seven
>Ex: *Seven Axel Ace*

Seveno
>Ex: *Seveno D Sorrentino*

Shad
>Ex: *Shad Weiman Marcson*

Shadow
>Ex: *Shadow Weiss*

Sharkey
>Ex: *Sharkey Plattes*

Shamiram
> Ex: *Shamiram Ruth Rachele Feinglass*

Sherlock
> Ex: *Rolland Sherlock Calliston*

Shiso
> (SHE-SO)
> Ex: *Shiso Sugato*

Shulamith
> Ex: *Shulamith Sayad*

Shushan
> Ex: *Shushan Sena Venaya*

Silver
> Ex: *Silver Trax*

Sin

> Ex: *Sin Sirocco*

Sinclair
> Ex: *Jackson Sinclair Marteno*

Sisal
> (SIGH-SUL)
> Ex: *Sisal Linden Ascot*

Sisiphus
> Ex: *Hale Sisiphus Waldron*

Sistina
> Ex: *Sistina Louisse Mirranta*

Skidmore
> Ex: *Skidmore Chains*

Sky
> Ex: *Sky Ryan Robetson*

Slade
> Ex: *Slade Jones*

Snow
> Ex: *Snow O Holday*

Soire
> (SWAR)
> Ex: *Soire Keats*

Sola

Ex: *Sola Terra DeCarta*

Solice

Ex: *Rebecca Solice Rite*

Solin

Ex: *Solin Marston Bessento*

Solito

Ex: *Solito Toma Bentayno*

Sonnet

Ex: *Sonnet Stark*

Sorrell

Ex: *Sorrell C Axton*

Sota

Ex: *Sota Phillips*

Sotelo

Ex: *Sotelo Viso Marketo*

Spanish

Ex: *Belinda Spanish Illes*

Spano

(SPA-NO)

Ex: *Seena Spano Wright*

Spasso

Ex: *Spasso Ray Gambino*

Spear

Ex: *Spear C Daye*

Spector

Ex: *Spector Mardin Ross*

Spenger

Ex: *Spenger Fishlin*

Sperry

Ex: *Sperry Halliday*

Spivey

Ex: *Spivey Ronald Karens*

Spruce

Ex: *Spruce Wexter*

Ssential

Ex: *Ssential Lace*

Stafford
>Ex: *Stafford Seyton*

Stag
>Ex: *Stag Cortin Foster*

Stallone
>Ex: *Davin Stallone Costelleno*

Stanislaus
>Ex: *Leslie Stanislaus Dellanto*

Star
>Ex: *Jack Star Frost*

Staten
>Ex: *Staten Jaron Maxton*

Stel
>Ex: *Stel C Yalene*

Steele
>Ex: *Steele Dane Lyndon*

Steinbeck
>Ex: *Hale Steinbeck Reese*

Steiner
>Ex: *Cole Steiner Waters*

Sting
>Ex: *Lace Sting Hallen*

Stinson
>Ex: *Stinson Price*

Stoli
>Ex: *Stoli Grayson*

Stolich
>Ex: *Stolich J Montanjo*

Storey
>Ex: *Storey Constance*

Stylo
>Ex: *Stylo Peretti*

Sulawesi
>Ex: *Carmen Salawesi Jay*

Sultana
>Ex: *Sultana Vey Spassovski*

Sumatra
>Ex: *Sumatra Boran Stelani*

Sumava
>Ex: *Sumava Riyan Allani*

Sumaza
>Ex: *Sumi Sumaza Sise*

Suname
>(SUE-NA-ME)
>Ex: *Bailey Suname Nenzano*

Sutter
>Ex: *Sutter Ray Vilenos*

Sylvania
>Ex: *Lucille Sylvania Pearman*

Syra
>Ex: *Syra Rollans*

Syson
>Ex: *Syson Pakistan*

Syvil
>Ex: *Syvil Kay Tine*

Tabaccan
Ex: *Tabaccan Landow*
Tabora
Ex: *Tabora Lean Dassin*
Tacoma
Ex: *Tacoma Sareen Halen*
Tafati
Ex: *Tafati Voyani*
Taipei
Ex: *Taipei Nevira*
Taiwan
Ex: *Peri Taiwan Rin*
Takoma
Ex: *Takoma Rhodes*
Talisker
Ex: *Fenton Talisker*
Talkien
(TAL-KEY-EN)
Ex: *Torren Talkien Wayne*
Talla
Ex: *Talla Jeannie Corsaire*
Talon
Ex: *Talon Valen Lyte*
Tamarack
Ex: *Tamarack Jackson*
Tamarin
Ex: *Tamarin Barcowski*
Tamayo
Ex: *Tamayo Guterrez*
Tamloren
Ex: *Tamloren Phillips*
Tamorino
Ex: *Tamorino Jane Tollin*
Tangier
Ex: *Angela Tangier Barston*
Targa
Ex: *Targa Nellie Dinneo*

Taro
> (TARE-OH)
> Ex: *Taro Katofski*

Tasso
> Ex: *Tasso Yasmine Kaes*

Tatum
> Ex: *Tatum Hilliardson*

Taupe
> Ex: *Taupe Franksen*

Tavin
> Ex: *Tavin J Lawsen*

Tavira
> Ex: *Tavira T Rexton*

Tavito
> Ex: *Freddy Tavito Gaston*

Taxi
> Ex: *Taxi Dae*

Teha
> (TEH-UH)
> Ex: *Teha Jorinski*

Teal
> Ex: *Sean Teal Corman*

Tech
> Ex: *Tech Richards*

Tehama
> Ex: *Tehama Deuno Gonzales*

Tellar
> Ex: *Tellar Axton*

Telly
> Ex: *Telly Lean Viceroy*

Tempela
> Ex: *Annie Tempela Jorlan*

Tennesse
> Ex: *Tennessee Ray*

Teno
> (TAY-NO)
> Ex: *Teno Raston Marker*

T

Teruko
> (TEH-ROO-KO)
> Ex: *Teruko Shohara*

Thelonius
> Ex: *Thelonius Mullen*

Tiago
> Ex: *Tiago Martin Rondejo*

Tibet
> Ex: *Tibet C Williamson*

Tice
> Ex: *Tice Jester*

Tide
> Ex: *Karen Tide Kingston*

Tiental
> Ex: *Tiental O Cayne*

Tier
> Ex: *Tier Lily Kates*

Tiller
> Ex: *Tiller Pollen*

Timo
> Ex: *Timo Escar Sevilla*

Tivoli
> Ex: *Tivoli Vince Terrani*

Tobiko
> Ex: *Tobiko Takara*

Tobler
> Ex: *Tobler C Rochanis*

Tohara
> Ex: *Tohara Hamoto*

Tokyo
> Ex: *Toyko Litton*

Toland
> Ex: *Toland Barrister*

Tommaso
> Ex: *Tommaso Paesano*

Tonara
> Ex: *Tonara Loreen Marbella*

Tonic
> Ex: *Tonic Laston*

Tonix
> Ex: *Warren Tonix Saitlin*

Toon
> Ex: *Toon Phillips*

Topeka
> Ex: *Topeka Anderson*

Torin
> Ex: *Torin C Alton*

Torina
> Ex: *Torina Maria Sandara*

Torino
> Ex: *Torino Cavello Sallenka*

Torious
> Ex: *Torious Jakes*

Toro
> Ex: *Astin Toro Kaye*

Toronto
> Ex: *Toronto Jones*

Totem
> Ex: *Kyle Totem Wexford*

Town
> Ex: *Colin Town Akers*

Toy
> Ex: *Toy Lawson*

Toyon
> Ex: *Toyon Perrins*

Trinidad
> Ex: *Trinidad Jakarta*

Trinity
> Ex: *Trinity Peerson*

Triton
> Ex: *Triton Phillips*

Triumph
> Ex: *Triumph Banks*

Trocade
> Ex: *Jenna Trocade Lexington*

Tropic
> Ex: *Tropic T Iles*

Truin
> Ex: *Truin Willit Sallisten*

Tucson
> Ex: *Tucson Delana*

Tule
> Ex: *Westmore Tule Finland*

Tundro
> Ex: *Rootie Tundro Cabintor*

Tustin
> Ex: *Tustin Jamiesen*

Tye
> Ex: *Tye Bansen*

Tyne
> Ex: *Tyne Feldner*

Tzale
> Ex: *Tzale Gin*

Tzena
> Ex: *Tzena O Dio*

Tzeno
> Ex: *Tzeno Mex*

Tzore
> Ex: *Tzore Jenazzo*

Ukiah
   Ex: *Ukiah C Stevens*
Uma
   Ex: *Uma Dae*
Uni
   Ex: *Uni Tores*
Uson
   Ex: *Uson Elo Rae*

V
> Ex: *Perry V Landor*

Vale
> Ex: *Vale Santos*

Valen
> Ex: *Valen C Haleston*

Vallarte
> Ex: *Vallarte Mindez Nirello*

Vallerian
> Ex: *Vallerian Saston Tull*

Vancouver
> Ex: *Vancouver Blake*

Vanden
> Ex: *Vanden C Forriston*

Vanderlin
> Ex: *Vanderlin Sommers Hale*

Vangough
> Ex: *Samuel Vangough Li*

Varsi
> Ex: *Varsi Raddes*

Veany
> Ex: *Veany Petcoff*

Vecta
> Ex: *Vecta Sails*

Vector
> Ex: *Vector T Paston*

Vela
> Ex: *Vela C Jones*

Vellino
> Ex: *Vellino Marston*

Velliz
> Ex: *Velliz Kona Chodroff*

Velna
> Ex: *Velna Ashford*

Velo
> Ex: *Velo Martine Vultano*

Velox
    Ex: *Velox Hay*
Velutina
    Ex: *Velutina Sasskina*
Venetka
    Ex: *Ventka Petcoff*
Venice
    Ex: *Venice Bisset Cansora*
Venisson
    Ex: *Venisson Paynes Price*
Venora
    Ex: *Venora Helena Fernando*
Veranda
    Ex: *Veranda Carmine*
Verbena
    Ex: *Verbena Stills*
Verdict
    Ex: *Joran Verdict Jones*
Vermont
    Ex: *Vermont Roden*
Verona
    Ex: *Verona Addson Sainnes*
Versaille
    Ex: *Francoise Versaille Poirot*
Vestry
    Ex: *Lew Vestry Colton*
Vets
    Ex: *Vets Miller*
Vicari
    Ex: *Vicari Angelli*
Vidal
    Ex: *Vidal O Zella*
Vidalia
    (VY-DAY-LI-UH)
    Ex: *Vidalia Nellie Stoen*
Video
    Ex: *Video Poland Vice*

Vienna
    Ex: *Vienna Varten Marks*
Viera
    Ex: *Viera DeTano*
Vignette
    Ex: *Silvia Vignette Torena*
Villena
    Ex: *Villena Marie Belinda*
Villian
    Ex: *Max Villian Sine*
Ving
    Ex: *Ving Ellis*
Vinniki
    Ex: *Vinniki Sandokowski*
Vinyl
    Ex: *Vinyl Corman*
Vio
    Ex: *Vio Scallin*
Violeto
    Ex: *Violeto Ristino*
Viper
    Ex: *Jackson Viper Dyce*
Viridine

    Ex: *Viridine Kadir*
Visa
    Ex: *Visa Marie Ossenta*
Visala
    Ex: *Visala Tippes*
Visali
    Ex: *Visali T Celtorres*
Visalia
    Ex: *Raquel Visalia Monroe*
Visino
    Ex: *Visino Esco Voltirez*
Visoko
    Ex: *Visoko Perrino*

Visolo

Ex: *Visolo Poltani*

Vitaya

Ex: *Vitaya Reeds*

Vitro

Ex: *Vitro Hayes*

Vitron

Ex: *Vitron C Parsen*

Volley

Ex: *Volley Dayo*

Voxen

Ex: *Voxen T Morrison*

Wade
Ex: *Wade Harrison*
Waikawa
(WHY-KA-WA)
Ex: *Waikawa Loa*
Waikea
(WHY-KEY-UH)
Ex: *Waikea Lani*
Waters
Ex: *Price Waters Gatelyn*
Waymond
Ex: *Waymond C Barrister*
Wedge
Ex: *Wedge Morrison*
Weiland
(WHY-LIND)
Ex: *Weiland Price*
Weiler
(WHY-LER)
Ex: *Weiler Takston*
Wen
Ex: *Wen Eston*
Wesson
Ex: *Wesson Vexler Carrington*
Westcliffe
Ex: *Westcliffe Borlin*
Westville
Ex: *Westville Samuel Sinns*
Wexler
Ex: *Wexler T Bates*
Whitaker
Ex: *Jallon Whitaker Atkin*
Whitecliff
Ex: *Whitecliff Bryerson*
Wiana
Ex: *Wiana Willistine*

Wildes
    Ex: *Roscoe Wildes Koh*
Winford
    Ex: *Winford Mar Elston*
Winona
    Ex: *Winona Rachele Wicksford*
Winrich
    Ex: *Winrich Sailes*
Wisconsin
    Ex: *Wisconsin Perra Goldberg*
Wolf
    Ex: *Wolf Bekks*
Wren
    Ex: *Wren Stevens*
Wrex
    Ex: *Wrex T Besselton*
Wye
    Ex: *Wye Cyland*
Wykosa
    Ex: *Wykosa C Shores*
Wylie
    Ex: *Wylie Ceyoto*
Wyoming
    Ex: *Wyoming Mayes*

Xylene

(ZY-LEEN)

Ex: *Xylene Aced*

Xylo

Ex: *Xylo Sarres*

Xylose

Ex: *Xylose Deorta*

Yacht
> Ex: *Tara Yacht Walton*

Yamoto
> Ex: *Yamoto Yoshiro*

Yana
> Ex: *Yana J Broughten*

Yare
> Ex: *Yare Julus Astin*

Yeager
> Ex: *Yeager Tuldanich*

Yemen
> Ex: *Yemen Roconovitch*

Yolano
> Ex: *Yolano Deisina*

Yosemite
> Ex: *Yosemite Payes*

Yoshi
> Ex: *Yoshi Itano*

Yoshiko
> Ex: *Yoshiko Uchida*

Ysina
> Ex: *Ysina Marks*

Yucatan
> Ex: *Yucatan Ides*

Yukon
> Ex: *Yukon Orlands*

Yunnan
> Ex: *Yunnan Seeres*

Zagat
> Ex: *Zagat Emillsen*

Zahir
> Ex: *Zahir Rhodani*

Zaire
> Ex: *Zaire Aldens*

Zala
> Ex: *Zala Johnson*

Zale
> Ex: *Zale Corrinsko*

Zamora
> Ex: *Zamora Jones*

Zanella
> Ex: *Zanella Ferrintino*

Zarim
> Ex: *Zarim Khyan*

Zarina
> Ex: *Zarina Elline Wayla*

Zarino
> Ex: *Zarino Bestorrey*

Zax
> Ex: *Zax Baxford*

Zealand
> Ex: *Zealand Stanton*

Zein
> Ex: *Zein Wints*

Zena
> Ex: *Zena Seiles*

Zeni
> (ZEE-NEE)
> Ex: *Zeni Jetkin*

Zenith
> Ex: *Zenith Warrens*

Zeo
> Ex: *Zeo Beilind*

Zeppli
> Ex: *Zeppli Rhodes*

Zepplin
> Ex: *Zepplin J Doberlin*

Zimbabwe
> Ex: *Charlin Zimbabwe Moldeno*

Zimbor
> Ex: *Restin Zimbor Kales*

Zinc
> Ex: *Zinc Erriden*

Zinnia
> Ex: *Rachele Zinnia Larres*

Zipper
> Ex: *Zipper Kates*

Zircon
> Ex: *Zircon Tolberts*

Zirrinia
> Ex: *Zirrinia Leiberts*

Zito
> Ex: *Zito Martinello*

Ziziva
> Ex: *Ziziva Sonnet*

Zodiak
> Ex: *Seyla Zodiak Basin*

Zoot
> Ex: *Zoot Maxton*

Zuki
> Ex: *Zuki Barrington*

Zuni
> Ex: *Zuni Wilsen*

Zurich
> Ex: *Zurich Moreno*

Z

VALERIE HANSEN

The author with **Reznor Tolland Tyler Wellston**